ENHANCING TEACHING IN DIVERSE CLASSROOMS

A Research Proposal Presented to the Faculty of
Humphreys University

To order additional copies of this book, contact:
Xlibris
844-714-8691
www.Xlibris.com
Orders@Xlibris.com

ISBN: Softcover   978-1-6641-2680-0
        EBook   978-1-6641-2681-7

Library of Congress Control Number: 2020915897

Print information available on the last page

Rev. date: 08/26/2020

ENHANCING TEACHING IN DIVERSE CLASSROOMS

A Research Proposal Presented to the Faculty of
Humphreys University

RICHARD A. VASQUEZ

CHAPTER I

INTRODUCTION

Diversity is a variety of identities and experiences. A group of people refers not just to their racial or ethnic background, but also their age, language, life experiences through culture and education experiences. However, when educating a diverse classroom, teachers should know how to approach diverse students. Drake (1993) stated:

The schools of tomorrow may have to be more sensitive to minority differences. Many Blacks resent being lumped into a single racial grouping without regard for social and economic status. Similarly, Puerto Rico does not necessarily enjoy being labeled with Cubans and Mexicans as Hispanics. It is clear that Asian immigrants from Japan, Korea, and Vietnam are very different. All of these groups and subgroups want to retain as much of their culture as possible, which is one reason California provides instruction for connecting a gas stove of English, Spanish, Chinese, Korean, and Vietnamese. Diverse mixture provides challenges that ensure student success and student discipline. (p. 265)

Background and Setting

California K-8 classrooms are diverse driven and intended for well-rounded student achievement. Educators must be able to effectively prepare students for overall success. Addressing how the curriculum is presented in a diverse classroom can make or break the experience of students. Therefore, being prepared and creating positive efforts to understand how students think and feel can help develop growth for higher learning. Furthermore, building strong relationships with diverse students will break barriers that challenge students from learning. Drake (1993) affirmed that one way that teachers can receive assistance with their effort to address diversity in the classroom is to consult with advisory committee members, school liaisons, and parents; ask them to discuss aspects of the curriculum that they feel are positive with respect to diversity as well as those that are negative. Teachers should then carefully analyze and use the committee's recommendations. Further preparations for working with culturally and ethnically different students include reading literature on their culture heritage and political and economic development as well as being familiar with present day successes and problems of minority groups. (Drake, 1993)

Drakes study took place in a suburban school district in the Central Valley area of California. Report demographics like enrollment by ethnicity, enrollment by English Language Acquisition Status (ELAS) and Grade and California English Language Development Test (CELDT) were examined by the researcher.

This elementary school had a total enrollment of 514 students. Out of all these students, 80.2 % were Hispanic or Latino, 13.8% Asian, 3.3% White, and 0.4% Pacific Islander. However, the overall district was 44.9% Hispanic or Latino, 20.5% White, 17.7% Alaskan Native, 6.9% African American, 3.7% Filipino, 0.6% Pacific Islander, 0.5% Asian, 2.8% other race and 2.4% not reported. Data revealed that there were 6,093 English Learner (EL) students in the district, 19,351 English Only (EO) students, and 611 Initial Fluent English Proficient. These data evidence a prime example of diversity in the California public school classroom. (Dataquest, 2019)

Statement of the Problem

Teachers need to consistently and openly discuss diversity issues with their students in order to establish a better rapport with them. Such discussions help in making the students more perceptive for learning about different cultures as well as bettering the community as a whole. Reaching out to families and the community through these inclusive channels will help improve awareness and understanding. (Drake, 1993)

A key component to the solution is preparing instructors with the ability to better understand different cultures and how to effectively work with diversity. For example, once a student is motivated to learn about his/her heritage, he/she will be more likely to want to know about other nationalities (Dills, 2018). Thus, this will make learning enjoyable, relevant, and meaningful with real-life connections. Diverse classrooms should be creative, inclusive of all students, and give a welcome feeling. Students need to also be assured that instructors can carry out the correct information about their nationality. The most common problem is that instructors are not well educated on their students' cultural behaviors or learning norms to best support their individual learning needs (Dills, 2018). For instance, some Asian cultures instill in children that they should never look an authoritative figure such as a teacher in the eye as a sign of respect. This, in turn, could be misperceived by a teacher in American society that values eye contact for clear communication and as a sign that the student is actively listening.

Purpose

The purpose of this mixed method study was to determine what factors go into effectively teaching diverse classrooms in public education. The outcome of the study provided data from surveys and interviews on how instructors effectively addressed a diverse classroom and how they prepared themselves for a diverse classroom on a daily basis. The researcher aimed to shed light on how to improve achievement of students who are in diverse classrooms. Educators must learn what approaches are best utilized in the classroom to avoid discrepancies among students and families as well as to foster a sense of equity and social justice. The outcome of this research provided data on how educators foster a rich and diverse learning environment and effectively teach students from diverse cultural backgrounds.

Research Question

The following research question emerged as a result of reflecting on previous research.

1. Do California public school teachers feel adequately prepared to support diversity in the K-8 classroom?

Limitations of the Study

The following limitations to the research proposal on effectively supporting classroom diversity should be noted.

1. The study took take place over a short period of time. If the time frame were longer, more extensive data collection may occur.
2. The survey data collected was only be from a K-8 public school district in the Central Valley area of California. Therefore, results were not be generizable beyond that setting.
3. Interviews were collected from a convenience sample rather than a random sample.
4. The interview portion was conducted on less than ten teachers from a K-8 public school district in the Central Valley area of California. Therefore, results are not generizable beyond that setting.

Definition of Terms

The following are key terms which will reoccur frequently through this research proposal on how a diverse classroom can foster successful for all students.

Classroom. For purposes on this study, this encompasses a K-8 public school district classroom in the Central Valley area of California.

Culture. The customs, arts, social institutions, and achievements of a particular nation, people, or other social group (Merriam-Webster Dictionary, 2019).

Diversity. The inclusion of individuals representing more than one national origin, color, religion, socioeconomic stratum, sexual orientation, etc. (Merriam-Webster Dictionary, 2019).

Embracing. Accept or support (a belief, theory, or change) willingly and enthusiastically (Merriam-Webster Dictionary, 2019).

Multicultural. Of, relating to, or representing several different cultures or cultural elements (Merriam-Webster Dictionary, 2019).

Student Success. The true measure of student success is how well students are prepared to accomplish their current and future academic, personal, and professional goals through the development of knowledge, a sense of responsibility and self-reliance, and a connection to the college and wider community (Nazareth College, 2014).

Summary

Chapter I provided an overview on a significant issue in California public education: fostering an effective learning climate for an ever diversifying student population. The need for active motivation, support, and the ability to bridge families and communities to a positive school experience in a diverse classroom is a necessity for young learners. This study examined how K-8 educators are instructing, practicing, encouraging, and reflecting on diversity issues today in the context of effectively supporting all students in the classroom. Because diversity is prevalent across the state of California, the effort to make classrooms more effective is demanding and challenging for educators. In the following chapters, a review of literature is conducted in Chapter II and a method of procedure is defined for the study in Chapter III.

REVIEW OF LITERATURE

According to Mordechay, Gamdara and Orfield (2019), by the year 2045, the United States will become a *minority-majority* which is a nation where those currently categorized as racial minorities will comprise the majority of the populace. This means that many public school districts, especially at the elementary level, are at the forefront of America's rapid racial transformation. A quarter century ago, 7 out of 10 school-aged children were White, but today that number is less than 1 out of 2. California contains one of the largest populations for a diverse classroom. Since 1990, the 5-to-17 year-old Latino population has more than doubled. Increasing from 5.3 million to than 12.8 million, making up almost a quarter of the school-aged demographic. (Mordechay, et al., 2019)

However, diverse classrooms help students engage in learning about the world and provide a platform for new learning. As diversity becomes the norm in public classrooms, educators must have the skills for delivering good learning outcomes. Students that engage in a diverse classroom atmosphere will focus on acknowledging the facts about different social backgrounds, community living, culture values, and other differences from each other. Diverse classrooms support the process of accepting and understanding the diversity of people and their cultures. With the number size of diversity growing, educators need to be prepared in and out the classrooms. In order to achieve higher learning through diversity, the main goal is to insure knowledge about different cultures. Drake (1993) stated:

Teachers need to be aware of their personal attitudes toward culturally diverse students. It's necessary to have this awareness because one's attitude will be reflected in the instructional process. Creating a diverse classroom will allow students to feel safe and welcome. Categories of information presented in this chapter include the following: (1) Driving Diverse Classrooms, (2) Student Success, and (3) Embracing Diverse Strategies.

Driving Diverse Classrooms

Students need challenge and motivation daily. However, driving diverse classrooms will engage learning that will increase academic rigor beyond the typical textbook. When students are driven to fulfill their maximum potential, they are more prepared and developed for social learning. Drake (1993) in the development of an ideal classroom affirmed that teachers need to solicit the views of the students and other advisers who are sensitive to cultural differences. A helpful exercise is to have students identify information that is culturally specific. For example, a social studies class might discuss the issue of a bilingual education program to address the needs of Hispanics. However, creating *classroom readiness* will define how educators teach (Drake, 1993). Educators we must know the outcomes of one's classroom for understanding how to project overall student success. Although each school has its own challenges, there are basic changes that schools can make to better drive diversity classrooms such as making sure multiple viewpoints are represented on a topic.

According to Larocque (2007), the common belief is that the school principals are the driving force behind increased student achievement. Principles that engage themselves on campus and in the classroom can drive diverse students' success. The four points that help drive a diverse classroom are: (a) principal leadership that empowers the school, (b) parent and community partnerships, (c) data-based decision making, and (d) a celebration of culture and ethnic diversity (Larocque, 2007). However, peers, teachers, parents, and principles can challenge students to drive their motivation. Teachers are the key for influencing diverse students. Students need to see instructors as role models who can provide knowledge and support regarding diversity. (Larocque, 2007)

Henfield and Washington (2012) conducted a study that suggested several White teachers are inadequately prepared to work within multiracial classrooms, while pre-service teachers have expressed dissatisfaction with their preparation for teaching diverse students. This unfamiliarity with diverse students can leave teachers ill-prepared to function effectively in multiracial schools. They interviewed 37 participants:19 were females. (73%), 7 male (27%) and of that group, only 12 teachers (46%) which had previously received what they described as academic or professional development multicultural training. Participants taught at the school for varying amounts of time; for instance, one teacher taught at the school for only six months, while another taught at the school for 30 years. These teachers instructed several different classes including science, language arts foreign languages, as well as family and consumer science. (Henfield and Washington, 2012)

Furthermore, according to Drake (1993), America's call for excellence and equity cannot be answered except in a diverse and culturally rich environment. Such a mixture of students is sure to generate challenges related to diversity. These changes must be addressed in a way that promotes cooperation and understanding between people of all cultures.

Student Success

Terenzini, Cabrera, Bjorklund, and Parente (2001) examined the influence of classroom diversity and found that it may well be contextual, that is, conditional (or dependent) on the degree to which students interact with one another in course related activities. For example, interpersonal contacts among students in low diversity courses may well have a different effect on learning than similar contacts in medium-or-high diverse classrooms. However, students must know that the classroom is the place for success and growth for learning.

Lewis, Nishina, Hall, Cain, Bellmore, and Witkow (2017) conducted a study on 823 (45% boys and 55% girls; M_{age} = 11.69) public middle schools sixth graders examining how cross-ethic peer relationships influenced academic outcomes with this diverse sample. The researchers found higher end of the years GPA's in core academic courses for White, Black, Asian, Latino and Multi-Ethic students. (M = 2.80, sd = 0.96; range = 0.04) (Lewis et al., 2017). The researchers concluded that a diverse classroom provides communication, ethics, social behavior and interaction with others. Furthermore, diversity also provides reasonable and creative thinking as multiple viewpoints are considered.

Students also play an essential role in career preparation as well in a diverse classroom. Most students that enter job markets with diminishing concern for community or national boundaries must know the practices of a diverse environment. Helping students learn to collaborate and communicate with the different cultures and backgrounds found in the 21st century work environment will guarantee success and knowledge. (Dills, 2018)

Furthermore, Dills (2018) suggested students of color earn lower grades when enrolled in sections with greater proportion of students of color; these effects occur exclusively for students of color with lower SAT scores. "The researcher affirmed that allowing for nonlinear effects displays important nonlinearities for white students. At above average fractions of classmates of color, white students earn higher grades in sections with more students of color" (Dills, 2018, p. 304).

Embracing Diversity Strategies

Embracing diversity in the classrooms is the only way students move forward in their education. However, educators must utilize strategies that will enhance the role of student's daily academics. School programs can help students develop skills that trigger their thinking skills for learning. According to Robinson and Clardy (2011), teacher education programs should require field experiences in schools where there is cultural, linguistic, and cultural diversity among the students. Even though California credential programs integrate bilingual education and embed English-learner strategy training across the content areas, more may still be needed to effectively prepare new teachers.

It is a necessity to prepare teachers to address diverse student needs and to be accepting of their cultural and linguistic communities. Educators and teachers must remember to avoid the *bias trap* (Robinson and Clardy, 2011).

Thiederman (2012) noted that students are first learners and avoiding embarrassing or insensitive questions can insure trust and responsive answers. Remember that each individual is unique; what an individual student learned as a group may not apply to the person in front of you. Thiederman (2012) further cautions that when an individual meets someone who conforms to what one has learned, he or she must remind themselves that this is just one single person – others may not think the same. However, with this consideration, preparing teachers for acceptance in a diverse classroom will help build a relationship between students and educators.

Northwest Online (2017) stated, "By around 2020, more than half of the nation's children are expected to be part of a minority race or ethnic group" (p. 1). Therefore, embracing diverse classroom should be the number one priority for all educators. Students spend a significant portion of their day with teachers, classmates, teammates and friends. Although academic achievement is a high priority, society expects the educational system to prepare students to live as good, productive citizens. As the culture and heritage of the citizenry becomes more diverse, teachers must show their students the value of embracing this diversity (Northwest Online, 2017). This can be channeled through stronger social and emotional development programs as well as civics-focused curriculum integration.

Chapter II provided a literature review of how to embrace diversity in the classroom and teaching training needed to effectively teach a diverse group of students. Categories of information focused on diversity in the United States public education system include: (1) Driving Diverse Classrooms, (2) Student Success, and (3) Embracing Diverse Strategies. Chapter III examines the research methodology, data collection, and analysis.

CHAPTER III

METHODOLOGY

The purpose of this mixed method research study was to answer the following question:

1. Do California public school teachers feel adequately prepared to support diversity in the K-8 classroom?

The outcome of the quantitative research provided evidence of why diverse students often struggle in learning and seek understanding strategies that teachers are utilizing to effectively support a diverse classroom. Surveying instructors provided data regarding how well teachers embrace diversity learning as well as the preparation and support they receive from their district. The qualitative interview responses provided in-depth insight on teaching strategies for successful outcomes in a diverse classroom.

Research Design

This mixed method explanatory research design created better understanding of how educators can practice good teaching skills for diverse classrooms. Phase I, a quantitative approach, was based on survey results which were analyzed and transferred into percentages and bar graphs. This approach helped explain the outcome of teachers' responses from the survey. The researcher believed that a graph was a more detailed visual representation and gives better understanding of the study. The result of Phase I informed Phase II.

Phase II, a qualitative approach, used interview responses to embrace the outcome of the data from the survey. Participants gave deeper insight on perceptions regarding how to effectively support a diverse classroom setting. During Phase I, the quantitative phase, the survey was given to all the general educational classroom teachers in grades kindergarten to sixth grade at a suburban elementary school in the Central Valley area of California. Once all the surveys were collected, the researcher followed up with a subset of the educators who participated in Phase I to begin the interview process. Each teacher that volunteered was given the freedom to answer how they felt about the study and was treated with respect by the researcher. After all data was collected from the interviews, the results were analyzed and coded for themes. Both quantitative and qualitative phases were focused on the practice and readiness of teaching diverse classrooms and examined levels of support and preparation regarding the matter.

Participants and Sampling

In most districts in California, teachers lack the teaching skills and practices of teaching in a diverse classroom (Dills, 2018). The participants for the mixed method study were teachers at the elementary level, kindergarten to sixth grade. The researcher had selected this location and instructors because of the prevalent diversity demographics represented in the district. There are other districts that the researcher could have chosen, but the lack of diverse students was not optimal for this study's intent. Therefore, the chosen location provided sufficient data on how well teachers were prepared to effectively support a diverse classroom of students in the Central Valley areas of California.

Phase I was not randomized and based on a convenience sample where the researcher surveyed all levels and grades available. The surveys were voluntary and each participant could refuse to answer any of the questions on the survey. Phase II, the face-to-face semi-structured interviews, were also voluntary and utilized a convenience sampling as well. Interview participants signed a consent form to grant permission of the interviewee regarding participation and the request to audio record. If the participant declined audio recording, then only notes were taken by the researcher. Each interview question was identical and given in the same order. The researcher only interviewed the volunteers that responded 'yes' to the follow up interview in the survey.

Data Collection and Analysis

Expert Review

The researcher designed a survey for a suburban elementary school in the Central Valley area of California. The school selected has fostered culture awareness, engagement and inclusiveness, as well as can inform the study of what strategies and approaches a teacher utilizes for fostering effective learning in a diverse classroom.

The researcher included key demographic items for comparison data among the responses. Demographic items include: (1) How long have you been teaching? (2) What credentials do you hold? (3) Do you work in a highly diverse classroom? These questions enlightened the study of student involvement and created opportunities for improvement in a diverse classroom. Additionally, the questions helped to identify teacher readiness and levels of preparation. The 13 question survey was sent out for expert review to three seasoned elementary school teachers and one administrator. Each teacher was given instructions to provide feedback on the following: (1) grammar errors, (2) questions that may unintentionally contain bias, (3) feedback that could enhance the survey, and (4) any suggestions that could be added or corrected. The researcher did not receive any feedback other than the survey was ready to be sent out to prospective participants. However, the researcher's advisor made a few minor suggestions such as adding a consent paragraph.

Phase One of the Study

After the survey was refined based on Expert Review feedback to better understand teaching readiness in diverse classrooms, it was prepared to be sent out to all teachers at a suburban elementary school in the Central Valley area of California (See Appendix A). The survey was designed not to exceed ten minutes. Each participant could choose not to answer any questions he or she felt they were not comfortable to answer. Once all data was collected, the researcher has kept the records for six months in a locked file cabinet and then discarded them. School surveys were be collected and kept in an envelope. The elementary school had its own envelope, thus making it easier to manage the outcomes of the data collection process. The surveying process consisted of acknowledgment of the teacher participant. He or she provided information on credentials, experiences, and highest degree earned, as well as other information about the teacher's academic background. This allowed the researcher to better understand the training and experience the participant had working in a diverse classroom. The survey used a Likert Scale that ranged from "strongly disagree" to "strongly agree". The researcher also included a "neutral" thus reducing the potential for survey bias. Each surveyor circled only one best answer. Once all the data was collected, it was analyzed using descriptive statistics such as percentages, bar graphs, and any other relevant tables or figures.

Phase Two of the Study

An interview process took place after the survey process where the results of Phase I informed Phase II. Each teacher was given the opportunity to respond to a question in the survey asking if they would like to participate in an interview after taking the survey. During Phase II, the interview consisted of questions that were not on the survey but went deeper on the topic. The interview questions were more focused on how to embrace and enhance diverse classrooms and what can they do as teachers to create an effective learning environment in diverse classrooms. Phase II helped provide valid support and recommendations to how teachers can learn and celebrate their students' culture background as well as to create an inclusive classroom setting. The interview questions were coded for themes. Thus, this made the results easy to understand and provided information of how to increase learning in a diverse classroom. The researcher utilized a digital recorder for recording responses when given consent by the interviewee in addition to taking notes. The interviews lasted for approximately 10-15 minutes.

Ethical Considerations

Safeguards were established in every aspect as the researcher had chosen questions that are related to the researcher's study and worked with an advisor as well as an Expert Review Committee. All four major aspects for ethical consideration were provided within the survey and during the interviewing process. Each category defined ethical behavior such as: right to privacy, professionalism, honesty, and the right to refuse participation at any time. These guides helped the process for the research of the study. The answers were stored in a locked file cabinet and only analyzed when conducting data for the research project. The surveys and recorded interviews were destroyed six months after the researcher had finished the outcome of the research project. Each participant understood and was informed about the interview through a consent process so they could prepare for the interview and feel comfortable with participation.

Summary

Chapter III provided details about the research design, participants and sample, data collection and analysis for the two phases using a Mixed Method Explanatory Design, and ethical considerations. The researcher provided data and evidence regarding approaches and strategies to enhance diverse classrooms as well as be more productive and focused on building the student-teacher relationship. This study further sought to strengthen effective teaching skills and practices when working with diverse K-8 classrooms. It also helped promote students, parents, and community learning about and embracing other cultures.

CHAPTER IV

FINDINGS AND DATA ANALYSIS

Diversity learning can help develop new skills and create better classroom participation. The results of this study will signify how teacher enhance learning with diverse students in the K-8 classroom.

QUANTITATIVE FINDINGS

The first phase of this mixed-methods study of embracing diversity in the classroom focused on examining how teachers prepare themselves for a diverse classroom. A study with a Mixed Method Design which included two phases was utilized: (1) a collection of quantitative data using a twenty-five-question survey with descriptive statistics analysis, and (2) a second qualitative phase which included semi-structured interviews that were coded for themes. The purpose of this study was to seek understanding on strategies that support teachers effectively working in a diverse classroom.

A survey was refined based on Expert Review feedback to comprehensively assess how perceptions of teachers on training and approaches for enhancing success in diverse classrooms. Furthermore, it underwent an IRB approval process at the researcher's institution. The survey was utilized with a convenience sample because it focused on K-8 teachers in a suburban school district in the Central Valley area of California. The survey was provided to the school district office for review and approval. It was then sent electronically via email from the district office to teachers at selected school sites. Additionally, hard copies were provided to one principal at a school site in the same district who willingly volunteered to promote it among his or her teachers. Out of the 50 participants that the survey was sent to, 22 completed the survey. This constituted a 44% response rate.

Research Question

The researcher has identified one main research question and sub-questions to be addressed during this study:

1. Do California public school teachers feel adequately prepared to support diversity in the K-8 classroom?

Results from descriptive statistical analysis are discussed to identify how teachers utilize effective approaches for embracing diverse classrooms in the Central Valley area of California.

Findings

A descriptive analysis was conducted on the survey to identify how teachers enhance working with diverse classrooms. The survey also explored how teachers can be effected in the same area when diversity is a factor in the California public classroom. In the same manner, all teachers (100%) agreed that working with students and colleagues with different cultural backgrounds from their own is the norm and comfortable. This provided valid information that teachers are welcoming of diversity and that 78% of the participants are currently working in highly diverse classrooms. However, most teachers feel that receiving adequate training and resources from their district is lacking and more support is needed.

Most of the participants suggested that they receive little support in terms of resources from their district when supporting a diverse classroom. This shows that most of the teachers that were surveyed do not have proper materials for effectively teaching in a diverse classroom. The adopted textbooks provide generally relevant connections (82% strongly agreed or agreed), but the teachers felt they must still supplement posters and other helping tools to foster a welcoming environment that embraces student diversity. Additionally, 54% of the teachers also felt that leadership strongly embraced and supported diversity on campus while 40% generally agreed.

Not all survey results were uniform in response. When asked the question about how students are involved in classroom discussions regarding diversity issues in today's society, participants had mixed responses. While 63% strongly agreed or agreed, 27% were neutral on the topic and 9% disagreed. Furthermore, the survey was also clear about the influence of the continued need for more professional development.

Having a productive diverse classroom involves learning about current diverse events and news from across the world. This will allow for open-end-discussions, class participation, analyzing real student problems, and other advantages that will help students understand and value diverse cultures. Interestingly, only 64% made sure students were involved in these regular discussions on diversity in their classrooms while all participants (100%) affirmed that they foster a classroom that reflects learning about diversity.

The overall outcome of the survey was progressive with a desire to continually embrace and improve diversity efforts at the school site as well as provided information for the study that embracing diverse classrooms is important to student outcomes. (see Table 1)

Item	Strongly Agree	Agree	Neither Agree or Disagree	Disagree	Strongly Disagree
I work in a highly diverse classroom	47%	31%	4%	18%	0%
Working with students and colleagues with different cultural backgrounds from my own is comfortable.	64%	36%	0%	0%	0%
I foster a classroom that reflects learning about diversity.	55%	45%	0%	0%	0%
Leaders on campus support and embrace diversity.	33%	63%	4%	0%	0%
I am committed to on-going learning and professional development regarding the needs of diverse students.	54%	40%	6%	0%	0%
I receive adequate professional development and resources from my district on supporting a diverse classroom.	11%	45%	40%	4%	0%
The books and materials I use to teach reflect multiculturalism.	18%	64%	9%	9%	0%
Bridging the classroom to the community is important in promoting cultural awareness	59%	40%	0%	0%	0%
Students are involved in classroom discussions about diversity issues in today's society.	18%	46%	27%	9%	0%
I enjoy teaching and discussing diversity topics with students.	38%	40%	18%	4%	0%

Table 1

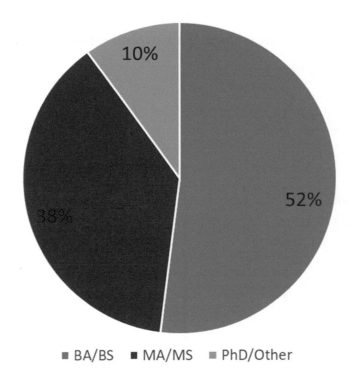

Figure 1. Highest Degree Obtained for Survey Participants

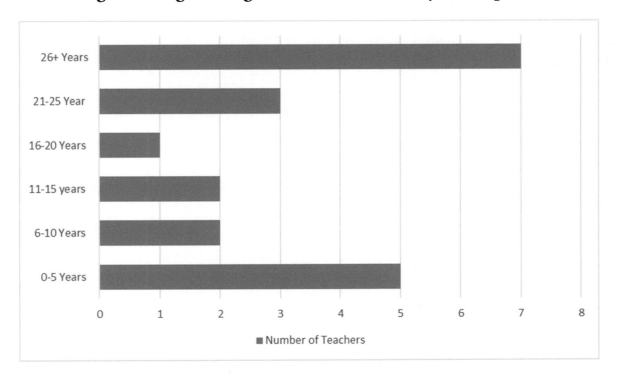

Figure 2. Years of Teaching Experience for Survey Participants

QUALITATIVE FINDINGS

The second phase of this mixed method study on effectively supporting diversity in the classroom focused on semi-structured teacher interviews for the portion of the study. Based on the results of the quantitative analysis reported earlier, interview questions were developed for K-8 teachers to describe perceptions regarding embracing diversity in the classroom.

Brief Overview of the Interview Process

Semi-structured interview questions were developed as a result of the data analysis from phase one of the study (see Appendix C). The purpose of the interview questions for the six K-8 teachers was to learn deeper perspectives and strategies for fostering diversity. The interviewers shared understanding of how teachers can create a welcoming environment for students of all cultures and interestingly provided their own unique description of how to support diversity in the classroom. Each was given the consent form and had the opportunity to view the questions prior to the researcher documenting the answers using hand-written notes as well as audio recording for transcription purposes. All questions were given the order presented and the interview took approximately 15 minutes.

Participants and Selection Process

The candidates selected for the interview process were volunteers from the Phase I survey. The last survey item asked if the participant would be interested in participating in a follow-up interview and if yes, to please leave an email address. The researcher communicated via email and set a time and date to meet on their school campus for the interview. Teachers often preferred to meet during their lunch hour. However, two of the six interviewees were phone interviews which were read the consent form and verbally agreed while audio taped prior to proceeding through the questions. The researcher met four of the six interviewees on campus. The time frame took two weeks. As seen on the chart below, the diverse array of teachers represented creates an opportunity for understanding strategies for embracing diversity in the classroom. Three teachers were from a charter school, one from public, and one private. All teachers interviewed teach within the Central Valley area of California.

Table 2 describes the demographics of the interviewees using fictitious names in relation to gender, grade level, years of experience, and diversity experience.

Table 2

Demographics of the interviewees in Relation to County, Training, Years of Experience, Grade Level, and School Type.

Participant	Place of School	Training	Years of Experience	Grade Level	Diversity Experience
Teacher A	Charter	credentials	20+	5th	YES
Teacher B	Charter	credentials	4	5th	YES
Teacher C	Charter	credentials	5	5th	YES
Teacher D	Public	credentials	2	K	YES
Teacher E	Charter	credentials	4	6th	YES
Teacher F	Private	credentials	3	6th	YES

Code Development and Application Process

The next phase of the application process focused on development of a code tree (see Appendix D). Each code and description represented a topic or idea from the transcripts. The code tree was initially designed by the researcher and an expert in the field to better understand the outcome of the interviews and how teachers employ approaches to supporting diversity. It was also intended to show how district policy, curriculum, and support can impact students in a diverse classroom setting. Values were assigned to each topic to indicate the range in perception of the participant. The process of identifying themes evolved with the initial use of color-coding participant responses. To identify the highest frequency of codes, a tally sheet was created after the color coding was applied to four transcribed interviews. The colors in the code tree give and understanding of how answers are common. The color codes that are shaded give better description of a response. The process revealed similar key points of focus and concern in the transcribed data for supporting diversity in the classroom.

Presentation of Code Occurrences

Table 3

Influences on Genera Education Teachers that Impact Successful Diversity Education Rank Order of Code Applications

Code Application Rank Order	Influences on general education teachers that impact successful diversity education
1	Teachers and student interactions (6)
2	Graphics and pictures that support learning (6)
3	Technology that enhances student learning (6)
4	Influence other than teachers and family (5)

The researcher identified the top four codes that influenced general educated teachers who are the K-8 teachers in the Central Valley area of California in this study (see Table 3).

The rank code provides valid information about how all teachers can agree on the topics listed above. Teacher and student interactions can help the process of learning. They all agreed that they liked interacting and engaging with students which makes the job fun and enjoyable. However, the majority suggested that homework and grading took time as well as was difficult. The most common perception that all participants suggested was that new instructors must seeking support from teachers and staff on campus. While all agreed on this sentiment, Teachers A, B and C stated that "seeking a mentor when starting a new teaching position, would help the development of how to teach and what not to teach. The support from other teachers, helps provide an opportunity for teachers to learn about their work environment." All affirmed that it's best to know how to direct students through mentorship if there has been no experience as a teacher. Teacher F suggested that providing exposure to students about diversity can lead to more critical thinking regarding diversity issues. Most of the interview participants suggested that exposure to diversity supports the process of learning. Furthermore, all participants believed that providing facts or current events issues about diverse cultures will increase the students' ability to participate in class and to develop a positive attitude toward diversity.

When utilizing graphs and pictures in the classroom it creates active thinking and helps students develop learning skills. All the teachers believe that pictures give a better understanding to how to solve issues. However, pictures are great learning tactics for EL students. The teachers also agreed that EL students are more responsive to learning when pictures are involved. The goal is to help students understand the language of learning through pictures.

Technology is a big part of learning and can motivate students to develop better communication, academic discipline, critical thinking and researching skills. Each interview participant spoke highly of utilizing technology in the classroom. Teachers B, C and D say that classroom do jo, helps students become more engaged, focused and shows success. The advantage of technology usage in the classroom is that students like learning from any source of technology. Technology is a learning curve for students that have a hard time with focusing on subjects such as: reading, math, science and other courses that are complicated.

The last category in the code tree is, influences other than teachers or family. When teaching we must realize that students learn outside of class that creates opportunities for new learning. Five of the six teachers say that students show their knowledge of learning from people that are influences other than family/teachers. These could be friends, community leaders, church members or activities such as sports. In any manner its best to utilize those influences to project an positive learning environment.

Summary

Chapter IV presented the quantitative and qualitative findings of a two-phase explanatory design study. Demographics of participants who completed the diversity survey and those who participated in a semi-structured interview were presented. Tables summarizing survey results, demographics of survey and interview participants, charts and the rank order of the code application were included. Additionally, findings will help identity effective approaches for embracing diversity in the classroom. Chapter V presents the discussion, implications and direction for future research.

CHAPTER V

DISCUSSION, IMPLICATIONS, AND DIRECTION FOR FUTURE RESEARCH

The purpose of this two-phased mixed methods explanatory study was to support diversity in the class and provide teaching strategies for new instructors. The study included two data collection points. Phase one consisted of a survey that was given through the district office to thirty K-8 teachers in the Central Valley area of California. There were 22surveys completed and returned. The survey participants are diverse and willingly volunteered for such research. (See Appendix A). Descriptive statistical analysis indicated significant findings. The key points in the quantitative data provided valid support on how teachers use similar strategies K-8 or think alike when approaching diversity in the classroom. Some major findings revealed that receiving adequate resources from the district has an impact on supporting diverse classrooms. However, data revealed that most teachers believe the district lacks interest when it comes to teaching diversity in the classroom. Phase two in the data collection included semi-structured interview questions that were developed as a result of the data analysis from phase one (see Appendix B). The focus of the interview questions for the six K-8 teachers was to further gauge perceptions regarding embracing diversity effectively in the classroom and what strategies teachers use to foster a diverse classroom. Each interviewee was selected using convenience sampling by the researcher and all are currently employed as educators in the Central Valley area of California. The interviewees have a range of teaching experience in a diverse classroom and are credentialed as well as have Bachelor of Arts degrees. Through the coding process, four themes emerged: (1) Teachers and student interactions, (2) Graphics and pictures that support learning, (3) Technology that enhances student learning, and (4) Influence other than teachers and family. The researcher used a triangulation of data for a holistic approach to the analysis as well as met with a trusted advisor on a weekly basis. Furthermore, steps to control inside bias included strategies such as good eye contact, speaking clearly, taking notes, audio recording for accurate transcription, and being responsive during the interview process.

Interpretation of the Findings

The results of this mixed methods study aligned with the literature review (Dills, 2018; Drake, 1993; Robinson& Clardy, 2011). Each reference gives proof to why diverse learning and teaching is important. The findings from the references listed above provides valid support to the research.

Research Question 1:

1. Do California public school teachers feel adequately prepared to support diversity in the K-8 classroom?

Based on these results of the study, the researcher found that majority of all teachers think in a similar manner when enhancing and supporting diversity in the classroom. Focusing on student progress, problem-solving activities regarding diversity topics, and open communication with students on cultures and diversity issues will help enrich a diverse classroom. The outcome for student success in a diverse classroom is to ensure common grounds of safety, fun and meaningful learning experiences promoting understanding and acceptance of diversity, good communication skills, and with support from the district, fostering an inclusive school culture. These strategies can support the process for higher learning or culture awareness in a classroom and school site. The data also gives good reasoning on how to approach EL students that struggle as English learners with grade level content such as the use of visual supports. Results from the data collection and analysis provided good detail of how to conduct a productive and inclusive classroom that is diversified as well as fostering understanding of what values are needed to embrace diversity.

Recommendations for Policy and Current Practice

Teachers and districts must have the same goals for enhancing diversity in the classroom. Having policies and practices in place for strengthening diversity learning will create culture productiveness. The recommendations based on the data shows that more interaction with district leaders can motivate teachers and community together with the evolving demographics for students in public and or private schools. The idea centered within the diversity policies should connect students that are from their culture as well as foster an inclusive and positive school setting. Linguistics and diversity success efforts focused on supporting English learners should be a key element in all school policies and receive appropriate funding for its efforts. The current practice or policy in the Central Valley area of California is not seen as favorable among teachers. It does not provide adequate support within the community and or administration. The on-going practices reported by K-8 teachers further indicate that there is an inadequate budget for supporting diverse learning or strengthening the curriculum to include diversity education and efforts. For example, it was reported that there are no or little diverse influences such as diverse guest speakers that represent the community.

Professional development trainings or workshops on how to better reach diverse students and their parents can help between community and administration. Purchasing learning materials focused on diversity curriculum for students can help the overall classroom environment, allow teachers to effectively teach, and create an understanding of different cultures that student face daily. For instance, technology is utilized daily for learning and enhances academics and could be favorably used among students with diversity curriculum as well. Therefore, seeking a budget for supporting diverse classrooms will give students a better outcome of learning. Furthermore, a diversity committee at each school site will provide good representation for all students and teachers as well as maintain accountability for diversity efforts.

Recommendations for Further Research

Students in diverse classrooms can build and achieve greater levels of empathy that will create a foundation for student involvement in the community and cultural awareness. Focusing on diversity learning will increase students' involvement and foster reflective analysis of themselves, their families, and people in the community. This researcher's recommendations for further research include a larger survey sample of teachers across California and to consider including high schools as part of the research sample. Thus, this would create a wider frame of study on how to enhance diversity in the California public classroom. A larger sample size will provide greater understanding among diverse groups of teachers and communities. Another aspect of further research is to conduct an analysis of funding that is potentially available for supporting diverse classrooms. Budgeting is a big problem for school districts and having the correct data to prove it will allow for better outcomes for all students and teachers.

Conclusions

The outcome of this research data has been interesting and provided significant findings regarding how students struggle in diverse public classrooms due to lack of support from their district. Furthermore, teachers struggle trying to find supplemental strategies and curriculum to enhance diversity learning in their classroom. All diverse classrooms provide a rich background of community and cultural living and provide detail of each student's character. The motivation of delivering good learning outcomes will help define and foster a student's ability to be productive in society or the community. The overall process to improve diverse classrooms in California is challenging due to educators not receiving adequate support of professional development trainings to teach such a class. However, the key element that must be addressed is that all students learn differently due to their unique cultural and ethnic background as well as their individual experiences. Once we understand as teachers how to effectively communicate with students regarding diversity, then students can grow and learn as a classroom community. The outcome for learning about different cultures can lead to success and leadership later in life. However, collaborating with families, teaching staff, and district administration on the matter will present greater outcomes. In conclusion, the data and information within the scope of this research has reasonable viewpoints from a teacher's perspective to better support diversity efforts to positively impact student success efforts. Teachers are genuinely eager to teach about diversity during the daily task of teaching because it helps students learn about new experiences in life. Gathering information about diverse groups will enhance the students' ability to actualize and professionalize their goals as they move through their schooling and their future careers. Classrooms are made for learning and engagement. The influence of teachers, parents, and district administration will provide a road map to all students that seek diverse educational learning.

REFERENCES

Dills, A. K. (2018). Classroom diversity and academic outcomes. *Economic Inquiry, 56*(1), 304-315.

Drake, D. (1993). Student diversity: Implications for classroom teachers. *Clearing House, 66*(5), 264-266. doi:10.1080/00098655.1993.9955988

Nazareth College Dictionary (2014). Definition of student success. Retrieved from https://www2.naz.edu/files/3614/1659/5956/Student_Success_Full_Definition.pdf

Northwest Online. (2017, October 20). *Embrace diversity in the classroom.* Retrieved from https://online.nwmissouri.edu/articles/education/embrace-diversity-in-classroom.aspx

Henfield, M. S., & Washington, A. R. (2012). "I want to do the right thing but what is it?": White teachers experiences with African American students. *The Journal of Negro Education, 81*(2), 148-161.

Larocque, M. (2007). Closing the achievement gap: The experience of a middle school. *Clearing House, 80*(4),157-162. doi:10.3200/TCHS.80.4.157-162

Lewis, J. A., Nishina, A., Hall, A. R., Chain, S., Bellmore, A., & Witkow, M. R. (2017, May 29). Early adolescents' peer experience with ethnic diversity in middle school: Implications for academic outcomes. doi:10.1007/s10964-017-0697-1

Merriam-Webster. (2019). Merriam-Webster online dictionary.Retrieved from https://www.dictionary.com/browse/webster

Mordechay, K., Gamdara, P., & Orfield, G. (2019, April). Embracing the effects of demographic change. *Educational Leadership, 76*(7), 34-40.

Robinson, C. C., & Clardy, P. (2011). It ain't what you say, it's how you say it: Linguistic and cultural diversity in the classroom. *Journal of Cultural Diversity, 18*(3), 101-110.

Terenzini, P. T., Cabrera, A. F., Colbeck, C. L., Bjorklund, S. A., & Parente, J. M. (2001). Racial and ethnic diversity in the classroom. *The Journal of Higher Education, 72*(5), 509-530.

Thiederman, S. B. (2012). *The diversity and inclusion handbook.* Flower Mound, TX: Walk the Talk Company.

APPENDICES

APPENDIX A

EXPERT REVIEWED INSTRUMENT

Diversity Survey for Teachers

Dear Teacher,

The purpose of this survey is to collect general information on how K-8 teachers work with diverse student classrooms. This survey should only about 10 minutes to complete. Participants have the freedom to stop at any time during the survey. Your participation in this survey is completely voluntary and all responses will remain anonymous. You are also free to decline to answer any particular question that you do not wish to answer for any reason. Data will not be administrated in any other form other than to compete a research project at Humphrey's University for a Master of Arts program in Education under the advisement of Dr. Donna Roberts who can be reached at 209.235.2934 with any questions regarding the research project. Thank you for your time and cooperation.

Sincerely,

Richard Vasquez

Graduate Student

Please answer the following questions.

Years Teaching: _____

Credentials Held: _____

Highest Degree Obtained: BA/BS   MA/MS   PhD/Other

1. **I work in a highly diverse classroom.**

    Strongly Disagree   *Disagree*   *Neutral*   *Agree*   *Strongly Agree*

2. **Working with students and colleagues with different cultural backgrounds from my own is comfortable.**

    Strongly Disagree   *Disagree*   *Neutral*   *Agree*   *Strongly Agree*

3. **I foster a classroom that reflects learning about diversity.**

    Strongly Disagree   *Disagree*   *Neutral*   *Agree*   *Strongly Agree*

4. **Leaders on campus support and embrace diversity.**

    Strongly Disagree   *Disagree*   *Neutral*   *Agree*   *Strongly Agree*

5. **I am committed to on-going learning and professional development regarding the needs of diverse students.**

    Strongly Disagree   *Disagree*   *Neutral*   *Agree*   *Strongly Agree*

6. **I receive adequate professional development and resources from my district on supporting a diverse classroom.**

    Strongly Disagree   *Disagree*   *Neutral*   *Agree*   *Strongly Agree*

7. **The books and materials I use to teach reflect multiculturalism.**

    Strongly Disagree   *Disagree*   *Neutral*   *Agree*   *Strongly Agree*

8. **Bridging the classroom to the community is important in promoting cultural awareness.**

    Strongly Disagree   *Disagree*   *Neutral*   *Agree*   *Strongly Agree*

9. **Students are involved in classroom discussions about diversity issues in today's society.**

    Strongly Disagree   *Disagree*   *Neutral*   *Agree*   *Strongly Agree*

10. **I enjoy teaching and discussing diversity topics with students?**

    Strongly Disagree   *Disagree*   *Neutral*   *Agree*   *Strongly Agree*

11. **What strategies can you suggest that will enhance a diverse classroom learning environment?**

_____

_____

_____

12. **What have been your greatest challenges teaching a diverse classroom?**

_____

_____

_____

13. OPTIONAL: Would you be interested in a follow-up 15-minute interview to further express your views and present insight on effectively working with diverse classrooms?

If yes, please provide a contact email: _____

APPENDIX B

INFORMED CONSENT INTERVIEW

Thank you for agreeing to be interviewed as part of the educational program at Humphrey's University. Ethical procedures for academic research undertaken from Humphrey's institution require that interviewees explicitly agree to being interviewed. This consent form is necessary for us to ensure that you understand the purpose of your involvement and that you agree to the conditions of your participation. This interview will be recorded, only by your permission. However, the information collected will be protected from all inappropriate disclosure under the law. No publications or reports from this project will include identifying information on any participant without your signed permission, and after your review of the materials. You are free to stop the interview at any time. The interview should only take 10-15 minutes long. If the teacher exceeds to oversee the time limit that will beneficial to the students study.

Please sign to indicate informed consent for this interview experience.

_____   _____

Signature   Date

APPENDIX C

Interview Questions

1. In what ways do you think diversity is important to student's academics?

2. What challenges do you think you will face in working with a diverse classroom?

3. Explain what you believe to be an effective strategy to introduce diversity to students who have only experienced a limited number of cultures?

4. What is your past experience or training with diverse students?

5. What ideas do you have for educating students about diversity?

6. How do you try to get students to participate in class?

7. What do you think the best strategy is for teaching EL's?

8. Do you feel students' cultures affect the way they learn and respond in class? How so? (Example)

9. What do you like best about teaching? What do you like least?

10. What advice would you like to give to a new teacher coming into a school like this one for his/her first job?

APPENDIX D

Code Tree

Title of Code	Description	Frequency of Occurrence (*f*)
Teachers Prep	Positive or negative experiences with class preparation	3
Homework	Grading students work outside of school.	5
Classroom Technology	Technology that enhances student learning.	6
Collaborative Learning	Grouping students for learning.	4
Mentor	Supportiveness from teacher colleagues.	2
Coaching and Feedback	Strengthen teacher's knowledge of how to teach.	3
Visuals	Graphics and pictures that support learning.	6
Discussions • Culture • Current Events • Critical Thinking • Exposer to Diversity	Teachers and student interactions.	6
Modeling	Teachers become models for students.	2

Lessons and Curriculum • Books and Literature • Supportive Materials	Adopted from the State	3
Issues on Policies	Rules adopted by school District.	3
Influence at home or Family • Friends • Afterschool Activities	Other role models outside the classroom.	5
Community Influence • Church • Clubs or Sports	Influence other than teachers and Family.	4
Development of Self Identity • Students behavior • Characteristics of learning.	Allow students to seek their way of understanding and learning.	2

Printed in the United States
By Bookmasters